How Did We
Find Out About
Neptune?

The "HOW DID WE FIND OUT . . . ?" series
by Isaac Asimov

HOW DID WE FIND OUT—

How Did We Find Out About Neptune?

Isaac Asimov
Illustrated by Erika Kors

Walker and Company
New York

First published in the United States of America in 1990
by Walker Publishing Company, Inc.

Published simultaneously in Canada by Thomas Allen & Son
Canada, Limited, Markham, Ontario

Library of Congress Cataloging-in-Publication Data

Asimov, Isaac.
    How did we find out about Neptune? / by Isaac
Asimov ; illustrated by Erika Kors.
        p.   cm.—(The "How did we find out . . . ?" series)
    Summary: An account of astronomers' observations over the years
leading to the discovery of Neptune's existence.
    ISBN 0-8027-6981-0   ISBN 0-8027-6982-9 (lib. bndg.)
    1. Neptune (Planet)—Juvenile literature.   [1. Neptune (Planet)]
I. Kors, Erika W., ill.   II. Title.   III. Series: Asimov, Isaac,
1920–   How did we find out—series.
QB691.A84   1990
523.4'81—dc20   90-38771
                                                                        CIP
                                                                        AC

Printed in the United States of America

2   4   6   8   10   9   7   5   3   1

Dedicated to
Emily Bennetts Gerard and
Sarah Elizabeth Jeppson,
the newest addition

Contents

1
Uranus

IN ANCIENT TIMES, people noticed that most of the stars made the same pattern in the sky at all times. They moved across the sky, but all in one piece, so to speak. They were called the *fixed stars*, because they seemed fixed in place. They were fastened to the sky, it appeared, and turned with the sky itself.

There were, however, seven heavenly bodies that changed position from night to night and seemed to wander among the pattern of the stars. One of these bodies was the Sun, and another was the Moon. The other five were objects that looked like stars but were particularly bright. Today we call these heavenly bodies *planets* (PLAN-ets), from the Greek word meaning "wanderer." We know them, however, by the names

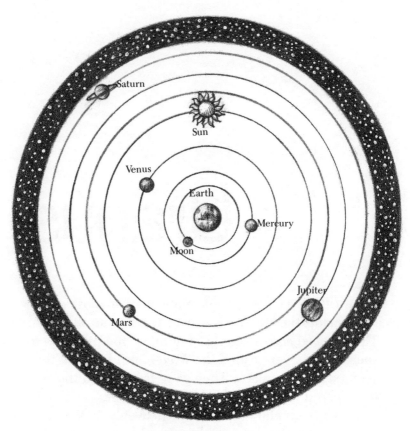

Fixed Stars
Ptolemaic universe

of the Roman gods Mercury, Venus, Mars, Jupiter, and Saturn. The ancient astronomers thought these planets (as well as the starry sky itself) all revolved about the Earth.

In 1543, the Polish astronomer Nicholas Copernicus (koh-PUR-nih-kus, 1473–1543) published a book in which he claimed that it made more sense to suppose that Mercury, Venus, Mars, Jupiter, and Saturn all revolved about the Sun. The Earth itself, he said, also revolved about the Sun. The Moon, however, revolved about the Earth.

Astronomers eventually accepted Copernicus's notion and began to apply the word *planets* only to the bodies that went around the Sun. These bodies were (in the order of distance from the Sun) Mercury, Venus, Earth, Mars, Jupiter, and Saturn. The Moon, going around the Earth, was Earth's *satellite* (SAT-uh-lite). All these bodies made up the *solar system* (SOH-ler SYS-tem). The word *solar* comes from the Latin word for *Sun*.

The telescope was invented in 1608, and it was quickly used to see things in the sky too dim to be seen by the naked eye. In 1610, the Italian astronomer Galileo (GAH-lih-LAY-oh, 1564–1642) discovered four satellites that circled Jupiter.

In 1665, the Dutch astronomer Christian Huygens (HY-genz, 1629–1695) discovered a satellite that circled Saturn. In 1672 and 1684, the Italian-born French astronomer Giovanni Domenico Cassini (ka-SEE-nee, 1625–1712) discovered three more satellites of Saturn.

Cassini was also the first, in 1672, to get a good idea of the distances of the different planets from the Sun.

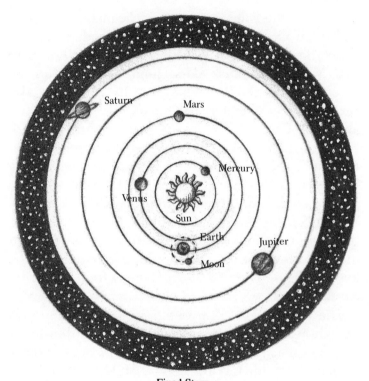

Fixed Stars

Copernican Universe

Saturn is 887 million miles from the Sun, nine and one-half times as far from the Sun as Earth is.

Right down into Cassini's time, and for a century more, Saturn was the farthest known planet. Astronomers didn't even imagine the existance of more distant planets, because it seemed that those farther planets would be seen if they were there. After all, all the known planets were bright and easy to see.

Then William Herschel (1738–1822), a German musician with a strong interest in science, appeared on the scene. He was born in Hanover, a portion of Germany ruled in those days by the British king. In 1757, he emigrated to Great Britain and became a successful music teacher in the city of Bath.

Although a musician by trade, Herschel had a passion for astronomy. He wanted to be an astronomer and study the stars and other objects in the sky. He couldn't afford to buy a good telescope, and he didn't want a bad one, so he decided to make his own. Herschel spent a great deal of time carefully grinding lenses and mirrors, and he learned how to do it so well that he ended up with the best telescopes in the world.

Once he had a good telescope, he began to study every object in the sky. On March 13, 1781, Herschel, as he kept passing from object to object, found himself looking at a tiny disk of light. Stars are always points of light, so the tiny disk could not be a star. Herschel thought it was a comet.

Herschel kept on studying it and noticed that the disk had sharp edges. That was odd, because comets always had fuzzy edges. What's more, the new object

Portrait of Herschel with the telescope he used to discover Uranus

moved against the stars very slowly. The farther an object in the solar system is, the slower it moves against the stars. This object was moving more slowly than Saturn, so it was farther away than Saturn, and no comet could be seen that far away.

Herschel had to conclude that he had discovered a new planet, the first to be discovered since the earliest days of civilization. It was 1,770 million miles from the Sun, twice the distance of Saturn. It was so far away that it was much fainter than the other planets. That, combined with its very slow motion, meant that astronomers didn't pay much attention to it even when they happened to see it.

An English astronomer, John Flamsteed (1646–1719), had seen the distant planet in 1690, but he just marked its position in his records, thinking it was only another star. A French astronomer, Pierre Charles Le Monnier (1675–1757), had seen it on thirteen different days in the 1750s. He had recorded each position, thinking it was a different star each time.

Herschel's good telescope and careful work settled the matter. It was a new planet. Herschel wanted to call it Georgium Sidus (The Georgian Star), after George III, king of Great Britain. Other British astronomers wanted to call it Herschel. A German astronomer, Johann Elert Bode (BOH-duh, 1747–1826), suggested, however, that they stick to names from the ancient myths, and astronomers decided to do so.

If we begin with Mars, the planet next beyond it is Jupiter, named after Mars's father in the Roman myths. The next planet is Saturn, named after Jupiter's father. Bode suggested that the new planet be called Uranus, after Saturn's father. This name was accepted.

In 1787, Herschel discovered two satellites circling Uranus and named them Titania and Oberon.

Other astronomers watched Uranus, too. They knew exactly how Uranus ought to move in its path, or *orbit*, about the Sun. In 1687, the English scientist Isaac Newton (1642–1727) had worked out his theory of gravitation. According to this theory, every object in the universe pulled at every other object with a force that depended on the masses of the various objects (that is, the quantity of matter in them) and the distances between them.

The Sun is by far the most massive object in the solar system, so its pull could be used to calculate the motion of Uranus. However, Jupiter and Saturn are quite large and at times are much closer to Uranus than the Sun is, so they produce pulls on Uranus large enough to affect its motion slightly. Measuring the pulls of the Sun, of Jupiter, and of Saturn, astronomers expected to be able to work out Uranus's orbit exactly. That meant they would always know the planet's exact position in the sky as it moved among the stars.

In 1821, the French astronomer Alexis Bouvard (boo-VAHR, 1767–1843) had been observing Uranus very closely. He plotted the motion of Uranus across the sky, using all the observations made by astronomers since the discovery of Uranus. He even used the observations of people who had seen Uranus and recorded its position without knowing it was a planet.

Bouvard found that Uranus was not moving in its orbit exactly as it ought to have been. By 1821, in fact, the actual position of Uranus was different from what it should have been by one-fifteenth the apparent diameter of the full Moon. That was not much of a difference, but it was enough to disturb astronomers.

Could something be wrong with Newton's theory of gravitation? Suppose the theory were adjusted just a bit in order to account for Uranus's actual path. Astronomers didn't want to do that, because Jupiter and Saturn, for instance, had orbits that fit the theory exactly. If the theory were adjusted to fit Uranus, Jupiter's and Saturn's movements would no longer fit.

Could it be that Saturn or Jupiter or both had different masses than astronomers thought, or were at somewhat different distances from Uranus than was thought? In that case, the pull of Jupiter or Saturn on Uranus would be slightly smaller or slightly greater than had been expected, and that might account for Uranus's not following its orbit exactly. However, no matter how carefully astronomers checked the mass and distance of Jupiter and Saturn, they could not account for Uranus's odd motion.

That left astronomers with only one other possibility. There was some gravitational pull they weren't counting at all. It would have to be a rather sizable gravitational pull, so it had to come from a large planet. If such a large planet were closer to the Sun than Uranus was, it would be brighter than Uranus and would surely have been seen.

The conclusion, then, was that the large planet would have to be farther from the Sun than Uranus was. If that was so, the planet would be dimmer than Uranus and would move more slowly, so it would be hard to see and recognize. If Uranus had not been discovered until 1781, it was no surprise that a planet still farther away, still dimmer, and still slower moving had not yet been found.

Then, too, a planet beyond Uranus might still be close enough to Uranus to pull on it and change its position quite a bit. It would be much farther from Jupiter and Saturn, however, and its pull wouldn't be strong enough to change the position of those planets noticeably. That would be why only Uranus, and not the other planets, traveled in a slightly wrong path.

If such a planet existed beyond Uranus, it ought to be found with a good telescope. Because it was so dim, lots of stars that were no dimmer would be surrounding it and drowning it out. Unless you knew in what part of the sky the mysterious planet was likely to be shining, looking for it would surely be a waste of time.

But how could anyone know where in the sky an unknown and unseen planet might be hiding?

2
Looking for a New Planet

In 1841, a twenty-two-year-old astronomy student named John Couch Adams (1819–1892) was studying at Cambridge University. He didn't have much time to himself, because when he wasn't studying he had to be teaching in order to support himself. However, he did have some time off during vacations, and he decided he would tackle the problem of the mysterious planet that might exist beyond Uranus and that might therefore be affecting Uranus's motion by means of its gravitational pull.

This is the way he went about it. Since Saturn is about twice as far from the Sun as Jupiter is, and Uranus is twice as far from the Sun as Saturn is, Adams felt that the new planet might be twice as far from the Sun as Uranus was. It might be about 3,500 million miles from the Sun.

Then, too, Saturn was smaller than Jupiter, and Uranus was smaller than Saturn. The unknown planet beyond Uranus must be still smaller, but it would not be tiny. It would still be several times as massive as Earth.

Suppose, then, Adams imagined a planet that far away from the Sun and that size. Where would it be, in the year 1841, to have been able to move Uranus slightly out of its path by just the amount that had been observed?

The unknown planet would have to be on the same side of the Sun as Uranus at this time, for if it were on the opposite side of the Sun, it would be much too far away to affect Uranus's motion in recent years. That wasn't enough. Adams had to calculate what motions the unknown planet would have that would just account for Uranus's motion.

The mathematical problem was very difficult, and most astronomers simply refused to tackle it. They felt they would be spending a long time at it and would not come out with any decent results. Adams, however, had the enthusiasm of youth, and besides, he happened to be the top mathematics student at Cambridge University at the time.

John Couch Adams

By mid-September 1845, Adams had finished his calculations, but he was an unknown young man and he didn't have a telescope under his control. He had to have someone who did have a good telescope and who would be willing to spend some time using the telescope and searching the sky in the place where Adams thought he might find the unknown planet. That wouldn't be easy, since there was a lot of work to do with telescopes, and no one would be overjoyed to use one for such a risky piece of work.

The two men who controlled telescopes in Great Britain were James Challis (1803–1882), the director of the Cambridge Observatory, and Challis's boss, George Biddell Airy (1801–1892), the Astronomer Royal. These were the two men that Adams had to interest. Unfortunately, neither Challis nor Airy thought there was any chance of locating a planet just by making mathematical calculations from the motions of Uranus.

When Adams brought his figures to Challis, therefore, Challis refused to help. He just told Adams to go to Airy with his work.

Airy was even worse than Challis. He was a very conceited man who always got himself involved with little things. He didn't have much of an imagination, and he treated all those who worked for him with contempt. The things he tried to do in astronomy always failed.

Somehow, Adams couldn't get in touch with Airy. This was before the time of telephones and telegraphs. He had to either send Airy a letter or visit him. Twice he visited Airy's home, but Airy was out both times.

The second time, he waited for him to return and then showed up again, but Airy was having dinner and Airy's butler refused to interrupt the astronomer.

Other astronomers who heard of Adams's work were impressed, but it was Airy who counted. When Airy finally got word of Adam's calculations, he was not really interested. Like Challis, he thought looking for a planet was a waste of time. He asked Adams whether his calculations explained something about Uranus's distance from the Sun, but Adams's calculations had nothing to do with that. Adams could see that Airy had missed the whole point of the work.

Adams was a rather shy and gentle person, and he decided that it was no use trying to get Airy interested, and that he would just never get anyone to use a telescope to search for the unknown planet. So he just gave up.

In France, meanwhile, an important astronomer named Dominique Franois Jean Arago (a-ra-GOH, 1786–1853) was looking for difficult problems in astronomy and interested in getting young astronomers to work at them, while he helped all he could. Unlike Airy, he was a friendly, outgoing person.

Arago grew interested in another French astronomer, Urbain Jean Joseph Leverrier (luh-veh-RYAY, 1811–1877), who was, like Adams, a very good mathematician. Arago asked Leverrier to investigate the orbit of the planet Mercury. It was a rather lopsided orbit, and Mercury's motions didn't quite follow what was predicted by the law of gravitation.

Leverrier went into the matter in greater detail than previous astronomers had. He carefully calcu-

Portrait of Urbain Jean Joseph Leverrier, in front of the
Paris Observatory

lated the pull of other planets on Mercury and showed that planetary pulls accounted for Mercury's motions almost exactly.

Leverrier's mathematical calculations impressed Arago, who then asked the young astronomer to tackle the even more difficult problem of Uranus's motions.

Leverrier got to work, going into the matter thoroughly. He collected all the observations of the position of Uranus, even those observations made before the official discovery. On June 1, 1846, he announced his final results, and they were almost the same as those that Adams had reached eight months before. (Of course, Leverrier knew nothing at all about Adams's work.)

The news of what Leverrier had done reached Airy in Great Britain, and this time Airy was interested. The fact that both Adams and Leverrier had reached the same conclusions made it seem that perhaps they were right. Airy, however, gave Leverrier all the credit and neglected to mention that Adams had done the same thing earlier. Perhaps Airy felt ashamed of having neglected Adams and preferred to pretend that Adams simply didn't exist.

Airy wrote to Leverrier and asked the same foolish question about Uranus's distance from the Sun, the question that had nothing to do with the problem. Leverrier was not the shy and quiet man Adams was, however. In fact, Leverrier was fully as egotistical and tyrannical as Airy. Leverrier wrote a letter to Airy telling him that his question was completely useless.

Leverrier's confidence impressed Airy, who instructed Challis of the Cambridge Observatory to begin a search for the unknown planet.

Challis, however, still wasn't interested. He put off the search as long as he could, because he was more interested in searching for comets.

He finally began his search on July 29, 1846, almost two months after Leverrier's work had reached Airy. Then, when he did begin, he didn't look at the spot in the sky indicated by Adams and Leverrier. Instead, he began the sweep of a large portion of the sky, because he had no confidence in the Adams-Leverrier figure's being correct. In order to complete the sweep, he would have had to study about 3,000 stars and see if any one of them happened to be in a position where no star ought to be, and if that star changed position from night to night.

Challis, with young astronomical students helping him, began his sweep and started noting down the position of all the stars seen. This was done mechanically and without close study to see if a position was recorded that should not have contained a star. After all, Challis wasn't really interested, and he didn't want to take the time for a really close and attentive look at each star.

As a matter of fact, on August 4 and 12, 1846, Challis's team had actually plotted the position of a star that was really the unknown planet. It was nearly where it was supposed to be, according to the calculations of Adams and Leverrier. However, Challis looked at it casually and failed to notice that no star should have been in that position.

3
Neptune

MEANWHILE, LEVERRIER WAS having trouble too. Like Adams, he didn't have a good telescope at his disposal and he couldn't seem to find any astronomer in France willing to make the necessary search of the sky. Of course, Airy had informed Leverrier that Challis was making the search, but the weeks passed and there was no word from Challis.

Leverrier, however, had received an astronomical paper a year earlier from Johann Gottfried Galle

(GAHL-uh, 1812–1910), a German astronomer who worked at the Berlin Observatory. Leverrier had thought the work to be very good, and he wrote to Galle on September 18, 1846, sending him his prediction as to where the new planet ought to be and asking him if he would make the necessary search of the sky.

When Galle received the letter, he wanted to undertake the search, but he needed the permission of the head of the observatory, Johann Franz Encke (ENK-uh, 1791–1865), and Encke was not keen to do it. He was afraid the search might be a waste of time. However, Heinrich Ludwig d'Arrest (dah-REH, 1822–1875), a young graduate student, who was present, joined in enthusiastically on the side of Galle.

As it turned out, that day happened to be Encke's birthday. It meant he wouldn't be at the observatory that night and wouldn't be using the telescope. He relented, therefore, and gave permission for the use of the observatory's very good telescope that night.

Galle and d'Arrest started looking as soon as it was dark. Unlike Challis, they looked at the very spot where Leverrier's figures showed the planet ought to be located. Just the same, they had trouble. They were looking for a little disk and weren't finding any.

D'Arrest then had the idea that they ought to get a star map of that region of the sky. The map would show the positions of all the stars, and they would only need to notice a star of the brightness the new planet ought to have that was not on the map. That would mean it was not a star but a planet that had now moved into the region of the map but had not been there when the map was made.

Johann Galle and Heinrich d'Arrest searching the skies for Neptune
in 1846

For that, a particularly accurate star map was needed. Otherwise, stars would be observed where they shouldn't be, simply because the star map was off in that particular case.

Galle and D'Arrest searched through the observatory files and came across a new star map that had been prepared with particular care and that happened to include the very area of the sky they were studying. They had not even known that particular star map existed.

They went back to work, starting all over. Galle peered through the telescope, calling out the position of each star he saw. D'Arrest was off in a corner with dim light (so as not to disturb Galle's vision) and kept saying that there was indeed supposed to be a star in that position.

In less than an hour, Galle called out the position of a star and D'Arrest, almost choking with excitement, said, "That star is not on the chart." The unknown planet had been discovered—on September 23, 1846. Galle and D'Arrest informed Encke at once, interrupting his birthday party with the best present he could have had.

The next night they looked again, and this time Encke joined them. There was no doubt. The object had changed position, and what's more, it showed as a tiny globe.

The news took a while to reach Great Britain. Challis was still looking, and on September 29 he spotted the unknown planet a second time. This time he noted it showed a disk. He wasn't sure, however, and he decided he would wait and look again the next

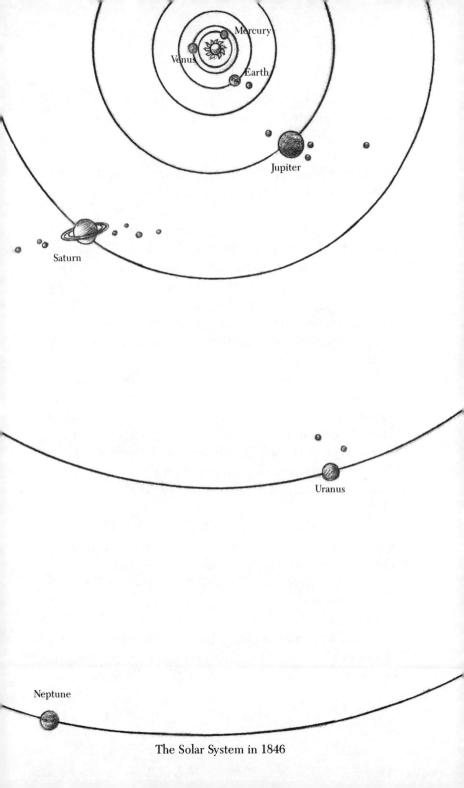

The Solar System in 1846

night with a better telescope. He wasn't in a hurry. The next night, September 30, the night was cloudy and he couldn't look.

On October 1, 1846, the news of the discovery of the new planet finally reached London, and Challis looked over his records and realized he had seen the planet twice and had missed it.

It was just like Challis and Airy, however, to each try to share the credit for the discovery of the new planet. Neither one mentioned Adams's calculations.

Fortunately, the British astronomer John Herschel (1792–1871), the son of the man who had discovered Uranus, publicized the fact that Adams had made the calculations also, and earlier than Leverrier, and had come out with the same results.

French astronomers objected that the British astronomers were trying to steal credit, but in the end Adams and Leverrier both received credit for their work. Both are now considered the discoverers of the new planet. Airy and Challis are remembered only for their stupidity and for their unfair treatment of Adams, who remained quiet and gentlemanly through it all.

When Challis died, Adams was appointed director of the Cambridge Observatory in his place. Then, in 1881, when Airy retired at the age of eighty, Adams was offered the post of Astronomer Royal. But he felt he was himself too old to take on the responsibility, so he refused.

There was some feeling, by the way, that the new planet ought to be named Leverrier for its discoverer. Leverrier himself was vain enough to think so. However, astronomers outside France would not have that. Because the new planet seemed to be a greenish blue in color, it was called Neptune, for the Roman god of the sea. That had actually been Leverrier's first suggestion.

One assumption that both Adams and Leverrier had made about Neptune turned out to be wrong. It had seemed natural to suppose that Neptune would be twice as far away from the Sun as Uranus was. However, it wasn't. It was only a little over one and one-half times as far away. Instead of being about 3,500 million miles from the Sun, it was only about 2,800 million miles from it. (Still, that's thirty times as far from the Sun as the Earth is.)

Then, too, although Neptune turned out to be smaller than Uranus, as had been thought, it was not smaller by very much. Uranus is about 32,500 miles in diameter, and Neptune about 31,400 miles. Each is a little over four times as wide as the Earth, so they are giant planets. However, their diameters are only a little over a third the diameter of Jupiter, the largest of all the planets.

Because Neptune is so far from the Sun, and because it moves so slowly out there where the Sun's gravitational pull is weak, going around the Sun once takes a long time. Neptune makes one circuit of the Sun in 164.8 years. In all the time since Neptune was discovered, it has not yet had a chance to circle the Sun even once. In fact, it won't come back to the spot in the sky where it was first discovered until the year 2011.

If it were possible for us to be standing on Neptune,

we would see the Sun as a fat point of light. The Sun would be too distant for us to make out as a little globe without the use of a telescope.

The Sun would still be the brightest object in the sky, however. It would be 450 times as bright as the full Moon is in our own sky. What's more, all that brightness would be concentrated into a point. That means looking at the Sun would still be dangerous, for it could still damage the eye.

Just as in the case of Uranus, Neptune had been sighted before its discovery by astronomers who didn't realize they were looking at a new planet.

On May 8, 1795, the French astronomer Joseph Jerome de Lalande (lah-LAHND, 1732–1807) noted a star whose position he recorded. He observed the same star two days later and found it had a different position. He thought he had made a mistake the first time, so he put down the second value and forgot about the observation. Actually, he had made no mistake. The "star" had moved. Once Neptune had been discovered, Lalande's records were checked and, sure enough, he turned out to have seen Neptune without knowing it.

It is even possible that Galileo himself had seen Neptune with his primitive telescope. At least he recorded a star that isn't there now, but Neptune was about there at the time he looked.

4
Near
Neptune

NATURALLY, ONCE NEPTUNE was discovered, astronomers began to study it closely.

By 1846, the year of its discovery, it was known that the Earth had one satellite, Jupiter had four, Saturn had seven, and Uranus had two. That was fourteen altogether. Of these, six were large satellites about the size of our Moon. These six were the Moon itself; Jupiter's four satellites, Io, Europa, Ganymede, and Callisto; and Saturn's largest satellite, Titan.

Since all the three previously known giant planets—Jupiter, Saturn, and Uranus—had satellites, it seemed

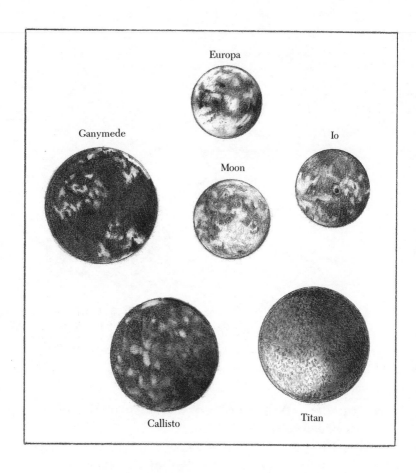

The six largest satellites.

that Neptune ought to have satellites, too. However, Neptune was so far away that perhaps its satellites would be too dim to see.

One British astronomer particularly interested in Neptune was William Lassell (1799–1880). He had heard about Adams's calculations, and though Airy was not interested, Lassell was. He had a very good telescope he had made himself, and he would have used it to search for the planet except that, at the time, he was in bed with a badly sprained ankle. By the time he was up and about and could have been observing, other matters had crowded in upon him and he forgot about Adams. It was another piece of bad luck for Adams, and was also bad luck for Lassell, who might have been the first to see Neptune.

Once Neptune was discovered, however, Lassell began his observations. On October 10, 1846, only two and a half weeks after Neptune had first been sighted, Lassell discovered a satellite of the planet. At least he thought he had, but the Sun was now close to Neptune's position, making the planet hard to observe. Astronomers had to wait until the Sun passed Neptune and was far enough on the other side for Neptune to be observed in the complete darkness of night. Finally, in July 1947, this could be done, and there was no question but that Lassell was right. Neptune did have a satellite.

(In 1851, Lassell went on to discover two more satellites of Uranus, which he named Ariel and Umbriel.)

Neptune's satellite was named Triton, after the name of the son of the sea god in the Greek myths.

Astronomers could tell little about Triton. Its distance was so great they could see it only as a dim point of light. Triton could not be magnified into a tiny globe so that its diameter could be measured. From its brightness and distance, however, and supposing that it reflected light the way other satellites did, astronomers decided that Triton was about the size of our Moon.

Triton was the seventh large satellite to be discovered. No other large satellite has been discovered since Triton was first seen, even though many small ones have since been sighted.

Triton circles Neptune at a distance of about 220,000 miles, almost the same distance from Neptune as the Moon is from Earth. Neptune, however, is larger than Earth and therefore has a stronger gravitational pull. So while the Moon travels about the Earth in twenty-seven and one third days, Triton travels about Neptune in not quite six days.

From the distance of Triton from Neptune, and the speed with which it circles the planet, we can calculate the mass of the Earth—that is, its weight, if we could imagine it sitting on a scale and being subjected to the earth's pull.

Although Neptune has a smaller diameter than Uranus, Neptune is one-sixth more massive than Uranus. Neptune is 17.2 times as massive as the Earth, while Uranus is only 14.6 times as massive.

Why should Neptune be more massive than Uranus even though Neptune is smaller?

Planets are made up of icy materials, rock, and metal. A volume of rock is heavier than the same volume of icy materials, and the same volume of metal is heavier still. A planet like the Earth, which is made up mostly of rock and metal, is massive for its size. A satellite like Callisto or Titan, which is made up mostly of icy materials, is light for its size. Supposedly, Uranus and Neptune are both made up of icy materials, rock, *and* metal, but Neptune has a bit more rock and metal in its makeup, and a bit less icy materials. Therefore, Neptune, although smaller in diameter than Uranus, is [more massive]. No one knows why this should be.

While Uranus and Neptune are among the giant planets, they are considerably smaller than the other two giants, Jupiter and Saturn. Saturn has a mass 5½ times that of Neptune and 95 times that of Earth, Jupiter has a mass 8½ times that of Neptune and 318 times that of Earth.

The Moon travels about the Earth from west to east. This is considered normal, since almost all the other satellites also travel from west to east. Triton, however, moves about Neptune from east to west. This is called *retrograde* (RET-roh-grayd) motion, from Latin words meaning "backward steps." No one knows why Triton moves about Neptune in this backward fashion.

For a hundred years after the discovery of Triton, no other satellite of Neptune was found. This was not surprising, since Neptune was so far away from Earth that any satellite smaller than Triton would be difficult to see.

In the 1940s, however, the Dutch-American astronomer Gerard Peter Kuiper (KOY-per, 1905–1973) was studying the distant planets. In 1947, he found that

Portrait of Gerard Kuiper with the McDonald reflector, with which he discovered Miranda in 1948

Saturn's largest satellite, Titan, had an atmosphere. It was the first satellite to be found to have one.

Kuiper also studied Uranus, which by then had four known satellites, two discovered by Herschel and two by Lassell. None of these is a large satellite. Titania, the largest, has a diameter of about 990 miles, less than half that of our Moon.

In 1948, Kuiper discovered a fifth satellite of Uranus, one that was closer to Uranus, and smaller, than the other four. This turned out to be about 300 miles in diameter, and Kuiper named it Miranda.

Then, in 1949, Kuiper discovered a second satellite of Neptune. He called it Nereid, which is the name of a group of sea nymphs in Greek myths. Nereid is about 350 miles across and is very difficult to see at Neptune's distance.

Nereid travels about Neptune in the normal west-to-east direction, but its orbit is unusual. Most satellites have orbits that are nearly circles, but Nereid travels about Neptune in an elongated ellipse. Neptune is located toward one end of the ellipse, so that Nereid is much closer to Neptune at the end than at the opposite end.

The average distance of Nereid from Neptune is about 3.5 million miles. At one end of its orbit, however, it is as close as 864,000 miles from Neptune. At the other end, it is nearly 9.8 million miles away. Nereid takes about 360 days to orbit Neptune.

To account for this peculiar orbit, some astronomers feel that Nereid must be an asteroid that approached Neptune too closely once in the far past and was captured by Neptune's gravitational pull.

In 1977, another startling discovery was made about the distant planets. On March 10 of that year, Uranus was going to move in front of a star. This was important, because as Uranus approached the star, the star would shine through Uranus's atmosphere for a little while. Then, when Uranus moved past it and the star emerged, the star would shine through the atmosphere again. Information about Uranus's atmosphere could be obtained during this time.

Astronomers studied the event from an airplane high in the air so that our own atmosphere would not confuse matters too much. The star turned out to blink on and off nine times before Uranus actually moved in front of it. When Uranus moved beyond it, the star blinked nine times again.

Uranus seemed to have nine rings of material that obscured the star. Until that time, Saturn was the only planet known to have rings. Saturn's rings, however, are broad and bright, while Uranus's rings are so narrow and dim that they can't be seen from Earth.

After that discovery, Neptune was watched very closely to see what would happen when it passed in front of stars. Astronomers decided there might be rings there, too, or parts of them at least. Starlight sometimes blinked on one side of Neptune, but not on the other.

5
Space
Probes

THE CHANCE OF SEEING detail, where Neptune was
concerned, was small. With the planet 2,800 million
miles away, little could be seen from Earth, even with
good telescopes.

However, the time was coming when astronomers
no longer had to watch Neptune only from Earth. The
space age began in 1957 when the first artificial satellite was placed into orbit about the Earth. By 1969,
the first human beings stood on the Moon.

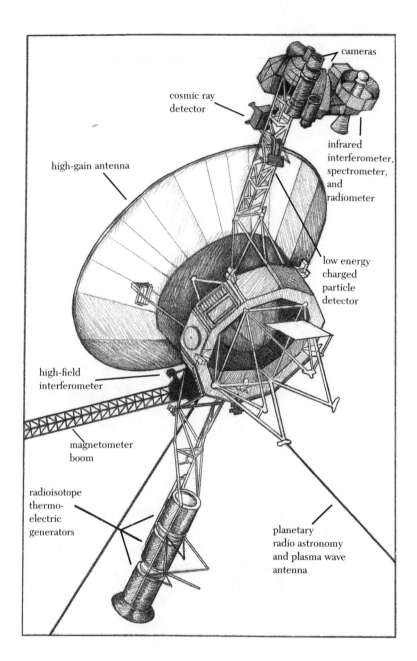

cameras

cosmic ray
detector

high-gain antenna

infrared
interferometer,
spectrometer,
and
radiometer

low energy
charged
particle
detector

high-field
interferometer

magnetometer
boom

radioisotope
thermo-
electric
generators

planetary
radio astronomy
and plasma wave
antenna

Voyager 2

Human beings have gone no farther than the Moon, but rocket probes have been fired to the planets. No human beings were aboard, but the probes carried instruments that could take photographs and make all sorts of measurements that could then be sent back to Earth.

In the 1960s, probes passed near Venus and Mars. Eventually, some even landed on the surface of those planets. One probe photographed Mercury from close up, and in 1986 probes studied Halley's Comet when it passed the Earth.

In the 1970s, probes began to be sent outward beyond Mars to the giant planets. *Pioneer 10* and *Pioneer 11* were the first to pass near Jupiter and to make observations of that giant planet and of its satellites.

After that, two more probes, *Voyager 1* and *Voyager 2*, were sent out. *Voyager 2* was the most successful probe up till now. Not only did *Voyager 2* pass by Jupiter and Saturn as *Voyager 1* did, but it went on toward Uranus and Neptune and sent back photographs and measurements of both planets.

Voyager 2, which was launched in 1977, passed Uranus in January 1986, after a nine-year trip. Sunlight at Uranus is only 1/368 as strong as at Earth, but it was still bright enough for photographing Uranus and its satellites, though exposures of nearly two minutes had to be taken.

Uranus turned out to be a bluish planet with what seemed a very calm atmosphere. This was not surprising. Jupiter has a very active atmosphere, because it is much closer to the Sun; the Sun's heat drives the atmospheric action. Jupiter has vast winds that form belts of clouds. Jupiter has the Great Red Spot, a giant tornado big enough for the entire planet Earth to drop into.

Saturn gets only one-third as much heat as Jupiter does, since Saturn is farther from the Sun. It has less marked bands and isn't as stormy. Since Uranus gets only one-thirteenth the heat that Jupiter does, its atmosphere is quiet.

As *Voyager 2* passed near Uranus, it gathered information that enabled scientists to calculate that Uranus rotated about its axis in seventeen and one-half hours. This rotation period had only been guessed at previously. *Voyager 2* also showed Uranus's thin, dim rings clearly and found ten rather than nine.

Uranus's satellites were found to be made up of unexpectedly dark materials. That meant that to seem as bright as they do from Earth, they had to be a bit larger than the earlier estimates. Their surfaces were interesting and unusual, too. This was especially true of Miranda, whose surface was so jumbled that astronomers think that early in its history it underwent collisions that knocked it apart and that its pieces then reassembled every which way.

Voyager 2 passed on beyond Uranus and in August 1989 passed near Neptune.

The first thing noticeable about Neptune was that, like Uranus, it was blue, even a deeper blue in fact.

The surface of Neptune and of the other giant planets is not a solid surface. It is, instead, the top of a thick atmosphere. The atmosphere consists, in each case, mainly of the very simple gases *hydrogen* (HYdruh-jen) and *helium* (HEE-lee-um). These are color-less. Added to them, however, are small quantities of other gases that give the atmosphere a color.

Jupiter has a variety of other gases, and we're not certain what they all are, but they make its surface look brown, orange, yellow, and white. The big tornado on Jupiter even looks reddish, so that it is "the Great Red Spot."

Saturn is colder than Jupiter, being farther from the Sun, and some of the colored material in the upper atmosphere is frozen. For that reason, Saturn is paler than Jupiter and seems to be yellow and white.

In the case of Uranus and Neptune, all the material that produces the colors of Jupiter and Saturn is frozen, and the atmosphere is composed mostly of three substances that remain gases even at low temperatures of these distant planets. These are hydrogen, helium, and methane. Methane has a molecule made up of one carbon atom and four hydrogen atoms and on Earth is found in natural gas.

Methane as we see it in small quantities on Earth has no color, but when it exists in large quantities, mixed with hydrogen and helium, it is bluish. This is what gives the color to Uranus and Neptune.

In one important way, Neptune is quite different from Uranus. Uranus is a quiet planet because it gets so much less heat from the Sun that Jupiter and Saturn do. Astronomers expected Neptune to be even quieter than Uranus, since Neptune gets only two-fifths as much heat from the Sun as Uranus does.

This is not so, however, Neptune is a surprisingly active planet. The winds in its upper atmosphere tear

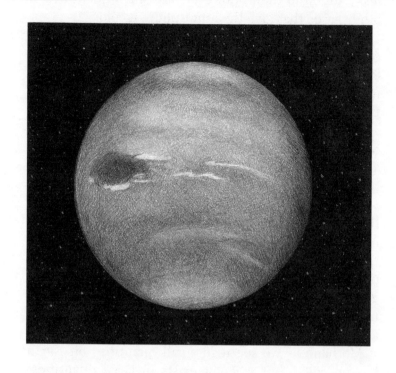

The surface of Neptune, showing the Great Dark Spot

along at speeds of up to 1500 miles an hour much faster than those on Jupiter. But Jupiter gets twenty times as much heat from the Sun as Neptune does. Where does the energy of Neptune's winds come from? Apparently, Neptune gets 2.7 times as much heat from its own interior as it does from the Sun. Why Neptune's internal heat is so high is still a puzzle.

Even more surprising is the fact that Neptune has a tornado that looks just like Jupiter's Great Red Spot and that is located at just about the same spot on the planet's surface. Neptune's tornado is smaller than Jupiter's, because Neptune itself is smaller, but it makes Neptune look just as Jupiter would look if that giant planet shrank. Neptune's tornado is blue, of course, and might be called the Great Dark Spot. By studying radio waves from Neptune, astronomers have found that Neptune turns on its axis in just a few minutes more than sixteen hours, so that it turns a little faster than Uranus does. The Great Dark Spot moves about the planet more slowly than that.

Why should Jupiter and Neptune both have these great tornadoes, when Saturn and Uranus don't? It should take a lot of energy to keep the tornado going, and we can be satisfied that Jupiter gets enough energy from the Sun for the purpose. But if Saturn and Uranus don't get enough energy to start a huge tornado, how does Neptune get it when it is farther from the Sun than any of the other three? Again, it is probably the result of Neptune's unusually large internal heat.

The probes that went into the outer solar system found additional satellites for each planet, satellites too small and dim to be seen from Earth. Usually, the satellites discovered were closer to the planet than the larger satellites we see from Earth.

Thus, Galileo first observed the four large satellites of Jupiter in 1610. In 1892, a fifth was discovered, smaller and closer to Jupiter than any of the first four. In the 1900s, eight tiny satellites were discovered far out from Jupiter, which were probably captured asteroids. That made fourteen satellites altogether. *Voyager 1* spotted three more small satellites quite close to Jupiter.

Saturn had nine satellites visible from Earth, but the *Voyager* probes spotted eight more small ones. Uranus had five satellites seen from Earth, but *Voyager 2* discovered ten small ones, all very close to Uranus.

Neptune was no exception. From Earth, astronomers had seen only two satellites, Triton and Nereid, but *Voyager 2* detected six small satellites quite close to Neptune.

In other words, before the probes went out, astronomers knew of thirty-three satellites altogether in our solar system. Now we know of sixty. All the new ones are tiny satellites, fifty miles across or less.

Another discovery involved rings. When the two *Voyagers* passed Jupiter, they discovered a single thin ring of dust and debris circling that giant planet. No one had ever seen that ring from Earth. *Voyager 2* then saw Uranus's rings. Astronomers were prepared to see rings around Neptune, too.

Sure enough, *Voyager 2* spotted three rings around Neptune. They were complete rings, but they were

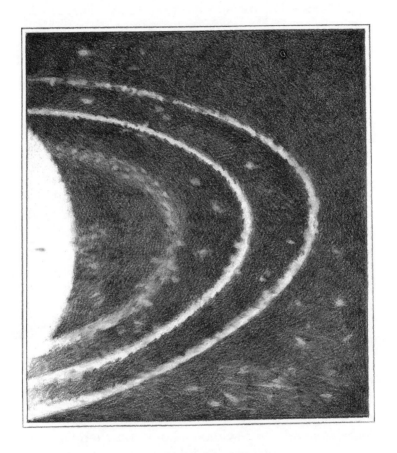

Neptune's rings

thin and clumpy. The clumps would hide the stars more than other parts of the ring would. That is why astronomers watching starlight fade in the neighborhood of Neptune thought incomplete rings might be there.

Now we know that three of the four giant planets have thin, dim rings. The question is: Why is Saturn the only one of the four giant planets to have large, broad, bright rings? What is so special about Saturn? Astronomers don't know.

When *Voyager 2* passed Saturn, it had a chance to study Titan, Saturn's largest satellite. It found that Titan had an unexpectedly thick atmosphere, as thick as Earth's or thicker, and made up of *nitrogen* (NY-truh-jen), which also makes up most of Earth's atmosphere. In addition, Titan's atmosphere contained considerable amounts of methane, which in the sunlight was converted to smoggy droplets of more complicated molecules obscuring Titan's solid surface (to the disappointment of astronomers).

Astronomers felt that Triton, Neptune's largest satellite, might have much the appearance of Titan. However, when *Voyager 2* passed close by Triton, they found it was considerably smaller than astronomers had imagined. Its gravitational pull was therefore less than Titan's, and it could hold only a thin atmosphere, about 1/60,000 as dense as Earth's. Its solid surface could therefore be seen clearly.

The thin atmosphere consisted of nitrogen and methane, as in Titan's case, and the surface was slicked with frozen nitrogen and methane, for Triton is a very cold world. Its surface is at a temperature of

Voyager 2 passes by Neptune as it heads out into deep space

about 370 degrees below zero Fahrenheit (or 223 degrees below zero Celsius).

The frosty surface reflects sunlight well, and it makes Triton seem brighter when viewed from Earth than it would appear if its surface were darkish rock. Astronomers, thinking its surface was dark, felt it must be as large as the Moon to appear as bright as it does. A shiny surface means Triton needs to be smaller to appear as bright as it does. In fact, Triton turned out to be only 1,700 miles across. It is still one of the large satellites, but it is the smallest of the seven. By comparison, our Moon is 2,160 miles across.

Cold as Triton is, it is still warm enough, under its surface, to turn frozen nitrogen into vapor. Frozen nitrogen underground seems to erupt into ice volcanoes now and then, producing craters and ridges.

Having seen all this, *Voyager 2* passed on beyond Neptune. It will continue to drift outward for countless millions of years. As far as we know, however, it will not pass near any astronomical bodies. Even if it does, it will have expended all its energy and be unable to send messages back to us any longer.

But it did a heroic job for twelve years, and we all salute it.

Index